9/14

Simple Machine Science

Inclined Planes

By Hope Collander

Gareth Stevens
Publishing

Please visit our website, www.garethstevens.com. For a free color catalog of all our high-quality books, call toll free 1-800-542-2595 or fax 1-877-542-2596.

Library of Congress Cataloging-in-Publication Data

Collander, Hope.
 Inclined planes / Hope Collander.
      p. cm. — (Simple machine science)
 Includes index.
 ISBN 978-1-4339-8132-6 (pbk.)
 ISBN 978-1-4339-8133-3 (6-pack)
 ISBN 978-1-4339-8131-9 (library binding)
 1. Inclined planes—Juvenile literature. I. Title.
 TJ147.C59 2013
 621.8—dc23

                                        2012018898

Published in 2013 by
Gareth Stevens Publishing
111 East 14th Street, Suite 349
New York, NY 10003

Copyright © 2013 Gareth Stevens Publishing

Designer: Katelyn E. Reynolds
Editor: Greg Roza

Photo credits: Cover, p. 1 Frontpage/Shutterstock.com; pp. 3–24 (background graphics) mike.irwin/Shutterstock.com; p. 5 ARENA Creative/Shutterstock.com; p. 7 David Leahy/ Digital Vision/Getty Images; p. 9 max blain/Shutterstock.com; p. 11 Sergey Lavrentev/ Shutterstock.com; p. 13 Goodshot/Thinkstock.com; p. 15 Christina Richards/Shutterstock.com; p. 17 iStockphoto/Thinkstock.com; p. 19 Hemera/Thinkstock.com; p. 21 Qba from Poland/ Shutterstock.com.

Printed in the United States of America

CPSIA compliance information: Batch #CW13GS: For further information contact Gareth Stevens, New York, New York at 1-800-542-2595.

Contents

Boldface words appear in the glossary.

What's an Inclined Plane?

Inclined planes help move things from a low place to a high place. They also help move things from a high place to a low place. You can find inclined planes in many places.

5

What Does It Mean?

A plane is a flat **surface**. A board can be a plane. "Inclined" means that something is tipped so one end is higher than the other. So, an inclined plane is a flat surface with one end higher than the other.

Going Up? Going Down?

Inclined planes make work easier. It's easier to move something heavy up an inclined plane instead of lifting it straight up. It's safer to move something heavy down an inclined plane instead of dropping it straight down.

9

Ramps Rock!

A ramp is an inclined plane. Ramps allow people in wheelchairs to get into and out of buildings. A parking ramp is a building where people park their cars. Parking ramps use inclined planes so cars can drive higher and lower.

11

Wheeeeee!

A playground slide is an inclined plane. When you sit at the top of a slide, **gravity** allows you to ride to the bottom. A flat slide wouldn't be much fun because you wouldn't be able to get moving!

13

Let's Get Moving

Movers use an inclined plane to move heavy things into a moving truck. They use the same plane to move heavy things off the moving truck. Using an inclined plane makes the movers' job much easier.

15

Dump It!

A dump truck can hold dirt, logs, rocks, and snow. When workers want to dump the load, they make the back of the truck tip up. Just like what happens on a slide, gravity causes the load to slide out of the truck.

Ladders and Stairs

Not all inclined planes are flat and smooth. Ladders and stairs are also inclined planes. One end of them is higher than the other. Ladders and stairs help people go up and down more easily.

19

Roller Coasters

Do you like riding roller coasters? If you do, then you're riding on some of the biggest inclined planes around! A **chain** pulls the cars to the top of the first hill. Then, gravity pulls the cars back down to the bottom.

Inclined Planes in Your World

- slides — **at play** — bike ramps
- **at play** — roller coasters
- ladders — **at work** — dump trucks
- **at work** — moving truck ramps
- stairs — **getting around** — parking ramps
- **getting around** — wheelchair ramps

21

Glossary

chain: a series of metal rings joined together that can be used like a rope

gravity: the force that pulls objects toward Earth's center

surface: a hard, flat area

For More Information

Books

Christiansen, Jennifer. *Get to Know Inclined Planes*. New York, NY: Crabtree Publishing Company, 2009.

Dahl, Michael. *Roll, Slope, and Slide: A Book About Ramps*. Minneapolis, MN: Picture Window Books, 2006.

Gosman, Gillian. *Inclined Planes in Action*. New York, NY: PowerKids Press, 2011.

Websites

Inclined Plane
atlantis.coe.uh.edu/archive/science/science_lessons/scienceles1/plane.htm
Try a fun inclined plane experiment.

Johnstown Inclined Plane
www.inclinedplane.org/
Learn about one of the biggest inclined planes in the world—a rail line in Johnstown, Pennsylvania.

Simple Machines
www.msichicago.org/fileadmin/Activities/Games/simple_machines/
Learn more about inclined planes and other simple machines by playing a fun online game.

Index